WISE QUOTES: BUDDHA

(174 BUDDHA QUOTES)

Rowan Stevens

TABLE OF CONTENTS

On Inspiration

On Life and Relationships

On Love and Gratitude

On Thinking

On Joy

On Meditation

On Peace and Forgiveness

On Wisdom

On Karma

On Change and Failure

On Anger and Jealousy

On Success

On Health

On Truth

Short Quotes

On Buddha

On Inspiration

If anything is worth doing, do it with all your heart.

There is no fear for one whose mind is not filled with desires.

Work out your own salvation. Do not depend on others.

A man is not called wise because he talks and talks again; but if he is peaceful, loving and fearless then he is in truth called wise.

Do not look for a sanctuary in anyone except your self.

To live a pure unselfish life, one must count nothing as one's own in the midst of abundance.

All that we are is the result of what we have thought.

If we fail to look after others when they need help, who will look after us?

One who acts on truth is happy in this world and beyond.

No one saves us but ourselves. No one can and no one may. We ourselves must walk the path.

There is nothing so disobedient as an undisciplined mind, and there is nothing so obedient as a disciplined mind.

Wear your ego like a loose fitting garment.

What you are is what you have been. What you'll be is what you do now.

When watching after yourself, you watch after others. When watching after others, you watch after yourself.

There is nothing so disobedient as an undisciplined mind, and there is nothing so obedient as a disciplined mind.

Give, even if you only have a little.

Drop by drop is the water pot filled. Likewise, the wise man, gathering it little by little, fills himself with good.

He who loves 50 people has 50 woes; he who loves no one has no woes.

Even death is not to be feared by one who has lived wisely.

Irrigators channel waters; fletchers straighten arrows; carpenters bend wood; the wise master themselves.

The greatest gift is to give people your enlightenment, to share it. It has to be the greatest.

If you knew what I know about the power of giving, you would not let a single meal pass without sharing it in some way.

Even as a solid rock is unshaken by the wind, so are the wise unshaken by praise or blame.

You yourself must strive. The Buddhas only point the way.

Nothing can harm you as much as your own thoughts unguarded.

Better than a thousand hollow words, is one word that brings peace.

Understanding is the heartwood of well-spoken words.

Ambition is like love, impatient both of delays and rivals.

Meditate... do not delay, lest you later regret it.

Ceasing to do evil, cultivating the good, purifying the heart: this is the teaching of the Buddhas.

People with opinions just go around bothering each other.

Delight in meditation and solitude. Compose yourself, be happy. You are a seeker.

If you find no one to support you on the spiritual path, walk alone.

Silence the angry man with love. Silence the ill-natured man with kindness. Silence the miser with generosity. Silence the liar with truth.

Ardently do today what must be done. Who knows? Tomorrow, death comes.

You, yourself, as much as anybody in the entire universe, deserve your love and affection.

If you propose to speak always ask yourself, is it true, is it necessary, is it kind.

Stop, stop. Do not speak. The ultimate truth is not even to think.

We are what we think. All that we are arises with our thoughts. With our thoughts, we make the world.

Just as the great ocean has one taste, the taste of salt, so also this teaching and discipline has one taste, the taste of liberation.

The one in whom no longer exist the craving and thirst that perpetuate becoming; how could you track that Awakened one, trackless, and of limitless range.

Endurance is one of the most difficult disciplines, but it is to the one who endures that the final victory comes.

Long is the night to him who is awake; long is a mile to him who is tired; long is life to the foolish who do not know the true law.

Whatever precious jewel there is in the heavenly worlds, there is nothing comparable to one who is Awakened.

Our life is shaped by our mind; we become what we think. Joy follows a pure thought like a shadow that never leaves.

Like a fine flower, beautiful to look at but without scent, fine words are fruitless in a man who does not act in accordance with them.

An idea that is developed and put into action is more important than an idea that exists only as an idea.

However many holy words you read, however many you speak, what good will they do you if you do not act on upon them?

Our theories of the eternal are as valuable as are those which a chick which has not broken its way through its shell might form of the outside world.

Chaos is inherent in all compounded things. Strive on with diligence.

On Life and Relationships

Live every act fully, as if it were your last.

Virtue is persecuted more by the wicked than it is loved by the good.

Nothing ever exists entirely alone; everything is in relation to everything else.

Purity or impurity depends on oneself. No one can purify another.

To support mother and father, to cherish wife and child and to have a simple livelihood; this is the good luck.

One moment can change a day, one day can change a life and one life can change the world.

She who knows life flows, feels no wear or tear, needs no mending or repair.

An insincere and evil friend is more to be feared than a wild beast; a wild beast may wound your body, but an evil friend will wound your mind.

Whatever words we utter should be chosen with care for people will hear them and be influenced by them for good or ill.

To be idle is a short road to death and to be diligent is a way of life; foolish people are idle, wise people are diligent.

Should a seeker not find a companion who is better or equal, let them resolutely pursue a solitary course.

If we could see the miracle of a single flower clearly, our whole life would change.

On Love and Gratitude

True love is born from understanding.

Radiate boundless love towards the entire world.

Love is a gift of one's inner most soul to another so both can be whole.

Let all-embracing thoughts for all beings be yours.

We will develop and cultivate the liberation of mind by lovingkindness, make it our vehicle, make it our basis, stabilize it, exercise ourselves in it, and fully perfect it.

Hatred does not cease through hatred at any time. Hatred ceases through love. This is an unalterable law.

Kindness should become the natural way of life, not the exception.

Speak only endearing speech, speech that is welcomed. Speech, when it brings no evil to others, is a pleasant thing.

One is not called noble who harms living beings. By not harming living beings one is called noble.

Being deeply learned and skilled, being well trained and using well spoken words: this is good luck.

Just as a mother would protect her only child with her life, even so let one cultivate a boundless love towards all beings.

In whom there is no sympathy for living beings: know him as an outcast.

Let us rise up and be thankful, for if we didn't learn a lot today, at least we learned a little, and if we didn't learn a little, at least we didn't get sick, and if we got sick, at least we didn't die; so, let us all be thankful.

On Thinking

He is able who thinks he is able.

It is a man's own mind, not his enemy or foe, that lures him to evil ways.

Delight in heedfulness! Guard well your thoughts!

Everything is based on mind, is led by mind, is fashioned by mind. If you speak and act with a polluted mind, suffering will follow you, as the wheels of the oxcart follow the footsteps of the ox.

A mind unruffled by the vagaries of fortune, from sorrow freed, from defilements cleansed, from fear liberated — this is the greatest blessing.

Know from the rivers in clefts and in crevices: those in small channels flow noisily, the great flow silent. Whatever's not full makes noise. Whatever is full is quiet.

You are a seeker. Delight in the mastery of your hands and your feet, of your words and your thoughts.

See them, floundering in their sense of mine, like fish in the puddles of a dried-up stream — and, seeing this, live with no mine, not forming attachment for states of becoming.

'As I am, so are these. As are these, so am I.' Drawing the parallel to yourself, neither kill nor get others to kill.

All experiences are preceded by mind, having mind as their master, created by mind.

To enjoy good health, to bring true happiness to one's family, to bring peace to all, one must first discipline and control one's own mind. If a man can control his mind he can find the way to Enlightenment, and all wisdom and virtue will naturally come to him.

All wrong-doing arises because of mind. If mind is transformed can wrong-doing remain?

What we are today comes from our thoughts of yesterday, and our present thoughts build our life of tomorrow: Our life is the creation of our mind.

The one who has conquered himself is a far greater hero than he who has defeated a thousand times a thousand men.

Transcendental intelligence rises when the intellectual mind reaches its limit and if things are to be realized in their true and essential nature, its processes of thinking must be transcended by an appeal to some higher faculty of cognition.

I will not look at another's bowl intent on finding fault: a training to be observed.

The external world is only a manifestation of the activities of the mind itself, and the mind grasps it as an external world simply because of its habit of discrimination and false-reasoning. The disciple must get into the habit of looking at things truthfully.

Mind precedes all mental states. Mind is their chief; they are all mind-wrought.

If with a pure mind a person speaks or acts happiness follows him like his never-departing shadow.

On Joy

There is no path to happiness: happiness is the path.

Happiness comes when your work and words are of benefit to yourself and others.

The enlightened one, intent on jhana, should find delight in the forest, should practice jhana at the foot of a tree, attaining his own satisfaction.

Thousands of candles can be lighted from a single candle, and the life of the candle will not be shortened. Happiness never decreases by being shared.

It is in the nature of things that joy arises in a person free from remorse.

Set your heart on doing good. Do it over and over again, and you will be filled with joy.

Do not dwell in the past, do not dream of the future, concentrate the mind on the present moment.

Should a person do good, let him do it again and again. Let him find pleasure therein, for blissful is the accumulation of good.

We are formed and molded by our thoughts. Those whose minds are shaped by selfless thoughts give joy when they speak or act. Joy follows them like a shadow that never leaves them.

On Meditation

Just as a candle cannot burn without fire, men cannot live without a spiritual life.

Looking deeply at life as it is in this very moment, the meditator dwells in stability and freedom.

Meditation brings wisdom; lack of meditation leaves ignorance. Know well what leads you forward and what hold you back, and choose the path that leads to wisdom.

Whatever a monk keeps pursuing with his thinking and pondering, that becomes the inclination of his awareness.

On Peace and Forgiveness

Resolutely train yourself to attain peace.

Indeed, the sage who's fully quenched rests at ease in every way; no sense desire adheres to him whose fires have cooled, deprived of fuel. All attachments have been severed, the heart's been led away from pain; tranquil, he rests with utmost ease. The mind has found its way to peace.

He who sits alone, sleeps alone, and walks alone, who is strenuous and subdues himself alone, will find delight in the solitude of the forest.

Do not turn away what is given you, nor reach out for what is given to others, lest you disturb your quietness.

*Those who are free of resentful thoughts
surely find peace.*

On Wisdom

*The fool who knows he is a fool is that much
wiser.*

*Whatever has the nature of arising has the
nature of ceasing.*

*Unity can only be manifested by the Binary.
Unity itself and the idea of Unity are
already two.*

*What is the appropriate behavior for a man
or a woman in the midst of this world,
where each person is clinging to his piece of
debris? What's the proper salutation
between people as they pass each other in
this flood?*

Let none find fault with others; let none see the omissions and commissions of others. But let one see one's own acts, done and undone.

The true master lives in truth, in goodness and restraint, non-violence, moderation, and purity.

Offend in neither word nor deed. Eat with moderation. Live in your heart. Seek the highest consciousness. Master yourself according to the law. This is the simple teaching of the awakened.

Life is like the harp string, if it is strung too tight it won't play, if it is too loose it hangs, the tension that produces the beautiful sound lies in the middle.

Do not believe in anything simply because you have heard it. Do not believe in anything simply because it is spoken and rumored by many. Do not believe in anything simply because it is found written in your religious books. Do not believe in anything merely on the authority of your teachers and elders. Do not believe in traditions because they have been handed down for many generations. But after observation and analysis, when you find that anything agrees with reason and is conducive to the good and benefit of one and all, then accept it and live up to it.

Just as treasures are uncovered from the earth, so virtue appears from good deeds, and wisdom appears from a pure and peaceful mind. To walk safely through the maze of human life, one needs the light of wisdom and the guidance of virtue.

The wise ones fashioned speech with their thought, sifting it as grain is sifted through a sieve.

The virtues, like the Muses, are always seen in groups. A good principle was never found solitary in any breast.

On Karma

Someone who has set out in the vehicle of a Bodhisattva should decide that 'I must lead all the beings to nirvana, into that realm of nirvana which leaves nothing behind'. What is this realm of nirvana which leaves nothing behind?

On Change and Failure

The root of suffering is attachment.

Nothing is forever except change.

There is no fire like passion, there is no shark like hatred, there is no snare like folly, there is no torrent like greed.

Both formerly and now, it is only suffering that I describe, and the cessation of suffering.

He who can curb his wrath as soon as it arises, as a timely antidote will check snake's venom that so quickly spreads, — such a monk gives up the here and the beyond, just as a serpent sheds its worn-out skin.

May all that have life be delivered from suffering.

It is easy to see the faults of others, but difficult to see one's own faults. One shows the faults of others like chaff winnowed in the wind, but one conceals one's own faults as a cunning gambler conceals his dice.

On Fear

The whole secret of existence is to have no fear. Never fear what will become of you, depend on no one. Only the moment you reject all help are you freed.

Those attached to the notion 'I am' and to views roam the world offending people.

There is nothing more dreadful than the habit of doubt. Doubt separates people. It is a poison that disintegrates friendships and breaks up pleasant relations. It is a thorn that irritates and hurts; it is a sword that kills.

Men, driven on by thirst, run about like a snared hare; let therefore mendicant drive out thirst, by striving after passionlessness for himself.

When one has the feeling of dislike for evil, when one feels tranquil, one finds pleasure in listening to good teachings; when one has these feelings and appreciates them, one is free of fear.

The instant we feel anger we have already ceased striving for the truth, and have begun striving for ourselves.

On Anger and Jealousy

You will not be punished for your anger, you will be punished by your anger.

Some do not understand that we must die, but those who do realize this settle their quarrels.

All tremble at violence; all fear death. Putting oneself in the place of another, one should not kill nor cause another to kill.

Anger will never disappear so long as thoughts of resentment are cherished in the mind. Anger will disappear just as soon as thoughts of resentment are forgotten.

I do not dispute with the world; rather it is the world that disputes with me.

They blame those who remain silent, they blame those who speak much, they blame those who speak in moderation. There is none in the world who is not blamed.

Those who cling to perceptions and views wander the world offending people.

Whoever doesn't flare up at someone who's angry wins a battle hard to win.

Do not overrate what you have received, nor envy others. He who envies others does not obtain peace of mind.

On Success

Neither fire nor wind, birth nor death can erase our good deeds.

Should you find a wise critic to point out your faults, follow him as you would a guide to hidden treasure.

As an elephant in the battlefield withstands arrows shot from bows all around, even so shall I endure abuse.

Praise and blame, gain and loss, pleasure and sorrow come and go like the wind. To be happy, rest like a giant tree in the midst of them all.

In separateness lies the world's greatest misery; in compassion lies the world's true strength.

Be a lamp for yourselves. Be your own refuge. Seek for no other. All things must pass. Strive on diligently. Don't give up.

Better it is to live one day seeing the rise and fall of things than to live a hundred years without ever seeing the rise and fall of things.

If you do not change direction, you may end up where you are heading.

On Health

Health is the greatest gift, contentment the greatest wealth, faithfulness the best relationship.

To keep the body in good health is a duty... otherwise we shall not be able to keep our mind strong and clear.

Without health life is not life; it is only a state of languor and suffering – an image of death.

The secret of health for both mind and body is not to mourn for the past, not to worry about the future, not to anticipate the future, but to live the present moment wisely and earnestly.

On Truth

Those who have failed to work toward the truth have missed the purpose of living.

Teach this triple truth to all: A generous heart, kind speech, and a life of service and compassion are the things which renew humanity.

There are two mistakes one can make along the road to truth...not going all the way, and not starting.

The calmed say that what is well-spoken is best; second, that one should say what is right, not unrighteous; third, what's pleasing, not displeasing; fourth, what is true, not false.

Conquer the angry one by not getting angry; conquer the wicked by goodness; conquer the stingy by generosity, and the liar by speaking the truth.

Three things cannot be long hidden: the sun, the moon, and the truth.

Short Quotes

Attachment leads to suffering.

May all beings have happy minds.

Born out of concern for all beings.

I am the miracle.

A jug fills drop by drop.

Every human being is the author of his own health or disease.

The tongue like a sharp knife... Kills without drawing blood.

The way is not in the sky. The way is in the heart.

On Buddha

To follow Buddha is to not follow Buddha.

Sven Schnieders

If you use your mind to look for a Buddha, you won't see the Buddha.

Bodhidharma

And the Buddha is the person who's free: free of plans, free of cares.

Bodhidharma

As long as you look for a Buddha somewhere else, you'll never see that your own mind is the Buddha.

Bodhidharma

Buddha means awareness, the awareness of body and mind that prevents evil from arising in either.

Bodhidharma

Buddhas don't practice nonsense.

Bodhidharma

A Buddha is someone who finds freedom in good fortune and bad.

Bodhidharma

Buddhas move freely through birth and death, appearing and disappearing at will.

Bodhidharma

But deluded people don't realize that their own mind is the Buddha. They keep searching outside.

Bodhidharma

To find a Buddha all you have to do is see your nature.

Bodhidharma

No one can force us to transform our minds, not even Buddha. We must do so voluntarily. Therefore Buddha stated, 'You are your own master'.

Dalai Lama

The color of the mountains is Buddha's body; the sound of running water is his great speech.

Dogen

The Buddha and all sentient beings are nothing but expressions of the one mind.

There is nothing else.

Huang Po

To awaken suddenly to the fact that your own Mind is the Buddha, that there is nothing to be attained or a single action to be performed. This is the Supreme Way.

Huang Po

The words of the Buddha offer this truth: Hatred never ceases by hatred but by love alone is healed.

Jack Kornfield

Respect Buddha and the gods without counting on their help.

Miyamoto Musashi

Even the buddha does not want anyone to follow him. Even the greatest masters cannot give you a single commandment. They see you so uniquely you, they see your freedom to be so uniquely for you.

Osho

Just two small things: meditation and let-go. Remember these two key words: meditation and surrender. Meditation will take you in, and surrender will take you into the whole. And this is the whole of religion. Within these two words Buddha has condensed the whole essence of religion.

Osho

There is no need for God! If you want to meditate you can meditate without God. Buddha meditated without God; he had no belief in God.

Osho

A Buddha is a Buddha, a Krishna is a Krishna, and you are you.

Osho

He taught virtue, mindfulness, and wisdom. These are the three pillars of Buddhist practice, as well as the wellsprings of everyday well-being, psychological growth, and spiritual realization.

Rick Hanson

If you cannot bow to Buddha, you cannot be a Buddha. It is arrogance.

Shunryu Suzuki

Buddha says there are two kinds of suffering: the kind that leads to more suffering and the kind that brings an end to suffering.

Terry Tempest Williams

You need to have confidence that you have the capacity to become a Buddha, the capacity of transformation and healing.

Thich Nhat Hanh

www.ingramcontent.com/pod-product-compliance
Lightning Source LLC
Chambersburg PA
CBHW071256070526
44583CB00017B/2491